SLAUGHTER
OF THE
INNOCENTS

A Morality Play

GLENN KUHNEL

The Peckwater Press

CONTENTS

INTRODUCTION i

CAST iii

ACT ONE, SCENE 1 1

ACT ONE, SCENE 2 9

ACT ONE, SCENE 3 18

ACT ONE, SCENE 4 26

ACT ONE, SCENE 5 34

ACT ONE, SCENE 6 44

ACT TWO, SCENE 1 51

ACT TWO, SCENE 2 58

ACT TWO, SCENE 3 66

ACT TWO, SCENE 4 69

ACT THREE, SCENE 1 76

ACT THREE, SCENE 2 89

ACT THREE, SCENE 3 103

ACT THREE, SCENE 4 113

INTRODUCTION

The gospel story of the slaughter of children by Herod is likely used by Matthew to make a comparison to the killing of Hebrew children by the Egyptian pharaoh since there is no historical attestation of the event. The episode is referred to as the slaughter of the innocents.

In his story Matthew used a quote from Jeremiah. "A sound was heard in Ramah, the sound of bitter crying and weeping. Rachel weeps for her children. She weeps and will not be comforted, because they are all dead."

While the gospel author created his story about slaughtered children, there have been countless disclosures of the sexual violation of children by priests. There are continued revelations of clergy betrayal and abuse worldwide.

Making these accounts even more shocking and appalling are the attempts by church leaders to hide and excuse these crimes. It seems that every week new reports of such conduct are reported.

Slaughter of the innocents is a story of secrecy and cover-up in the Catholic Church's attempt to shield itself from scandal and to protect members of the clergy accused of the sexual abuse of children.

Slaughter of the Innocents is about a mother's grief that uncovers the horrible truth behind her son's suicide; a priest faced with obedience to a Church he no longer has faith in; and a bishop intent on defending his church, no matter what.

In an effort to bring some sense of justice, the victims and their protectors use a forgotten medieval rite to chastise corrupt clergy to deal with the lies and deception of the bishop.

CAST

Michael O'Malley: Commentator and Priest Secretary to Bishop Robert Bergeron- Late 20's

Bishop Robert Bergeron: Bishop of Ste. Pierre-60's

Mrs. Patrick Lynch: Mother of a dead son-late 50's

Sylvia Rappaport: Criminal Investigator-30-40

Patrick Fairchild: Attorney-40-50

Walter Ashcroft: Attorney-40-50

Denis Frank: Victim of childhood sexual abuse-20's

Former members of Bergeron's Seminary Class-early 60's

Gordon Wadhams: Psychotherapist

John Fenton: A Judge

Franco Terranova: University History Professor

Henry Campion: A Businessman

Terry Fowler: Salesman

Voices of Victims: 10-12 Men and Women Victims

Priest in Confessional

ACT ONE

SCENE 1

SETTING: Bishop's Office. A desk and chairs. The space is opulent and pricey looking with appropriate religious art. Bergeron and O'Malley in clerics, wearing black suits, clerical collars. Bishop has pectoral cross and ring is seated at his desk. O'Malley's outer office is also visible. It has desk and office appointments.

AT RISE: O'MALLEY, in black suit, white shirt. Addresses the audience.

O'MALLEY

My name is O'Malley. Michael O'Malley and I used to be a priest...Well, I guess, "technically" I still am. You know, they said: "Thou art a priest forever" when I was ordained. And it doesn't come off because I've turned my collar around.

I guess I always wanted to be a priest. I fell in love with the Church and what I thought it stood for; helping people know what was right, leading

1

them to God, looking out for people who were put down.

And everybody told me how special it was that God had chosen me. I loved studying for a life of service. And I was incredibly lucky to be sent to the best universities to study theology. Many of the men I studied with never went on to ordination, but they are doing well, even good, as teachers, counselors, loving husbands and fathers.

It's not so much that I left the Church, I just found I could do more good in other ways. So now, I'm a therapist.

Anyway, after I was finally ordained, I got a "desk job" as secretary to my bishop in the Diocese of Ste. Pierre.

I'm pretty sure you've seen a lot of press and tv coverage about stories of priests molesting and sexually abusing children. Bad priests make good news. Now it's about bishops and cardinals, even the pope who tried to keep the whole thing quiet to preserve the respectable "reputation" of the Church they say.

I thought that you might be interested in what happened in the unimportant diocese of Ste. Pierre and why I became disillusioned with the Church. In a way, this is a morality play. And you know what they are about.

(Light fades on O'Malley and comes up on offices as O'Malley, now dressed in clerical rabat approaches the bishops' desk.)

O'MALLEY

That Lynch woman is here again, I told her you were busy and there's nothing you can do. She still wants to see you.

BISHOP

I told YOU I didn't want to be disturbed! And I told YOU to handle it!

O'MALLEY

I've explained that there's nothing we can do. Its' the law.

BISHOP

Well, tell her **again** and get rid of her.

O'MALLEY

Couldn't you just grant the permission? After all she's a grieving mother.

BISHOP

Grieving or not, her son's not getting a Catholic funeral.

The kid was a mentally deranged psycho who shot himself at Mass. The media coverage alone was enough! Now get rid of her!

(O'Malley leaves lights fade on Bishop's office and come up on an outer office and a middle-aged woman dressed in black is sitting in a chair. O'Malley walks to her.)

MRS. LYNCH

When Fr. Murtaugh said Eddie couldn't have a funeral Mass or be buried in blessed ground, I thought surely the bishop...

O'MALLEY

Mrs. Lynch, I'm afraid the answer is still no. The bishop will not override canon law. It's clear, a Catholic funeral must be denied to known sinners and the fact that Eddie committed suicide only makes matters worse.

MRS. LYNCH

What do you mean? Known sinners!?

O'MALLEY

The fact that Eddie shot himself at a Mass after shouting obscenities and something about the innocents should speak for itself. The act was a desecration of a church.

MRS. LYNCH

My son went to Mass every week. My son was an altar server til he was in high school. My son won a prize for religion. My son did nothing but help people all his life. The past few weeks he changed; something was bothering him. And now you tell me that you can judge him and condemn him and deny him a funeral? Whatever happened to mercy and compassion?

O'MALLEY

Mrs. Lynch, you may see your son as a good man. But what the church sees is a young man who killed himself during the celebration of Mass and blasphemed in public. That puts him 'outside' the church and puts us in an awkward position, if we say he can be given a funeral **in** the church. Do you understand?

MRS. LYNCH

Is this how you "respect life" by telling me that my flesh and blood is not worthy of your prayers?

O'MALLEY

I know you're upset.

MRS. LYNCH

Upset? Upset doesn't even come close. You don't know what it's like to lose a son. Mary must have known when she saw her son crucified for no reason.

O'MALLEY

Mrs. Lynch, I can't possibly know the pain of your loss.

MRS. LYNCH

But when I come to people who I believe can give meaning to the loss, you tell me that there's nothing you can do to give some meaning to (*Sobbing*) death. No, you deny sympathy and pity because it might send the "wrong" message! That's what you and the bishop are telling me! I've been a good Catholic all my life. I just don't understand.

O'MALLEY

Don't you see your son's action was sacrilegious and public, a whole church witnessed and heard what he said and did, taking his own life and desecrating a church.

MRS. LYNCH

I understand that my 19 year old son, who wanted to be a doctor, took his own life because there was something so horrible and hurtful that he couldn't face it and that somehow **where** he chose to end his life had something to do with it. And I understand that the church I have believed in all my life will not let him rest in peace.

O'MALLEY

I'm sorry, Mrs. Lynch, there's nothing we can do. And I hope this matter is settled.

MRS. LYNCH

No father, I'm sorry that my son's death has been such a scandal and inconvenience! (Mrs. Lynch gets up to leave then pauses.) One last thing father, I want you to hear **this** confession: I want you and your bishop to go to hell!

O'MALLEY

I know you don't mean that. You're upset and grieving and thought the church was the place to come, but there are laws and we must follow them.

MRS. LYNCH

Don't patronize me, father. I came to you because my son was sick and did something that I thought could be forgiven, but I was wrong. All you are interested in is using your rules to make the church look good.

O'MALLEY

Mrs. Lynch, I'm sorry, that's just the way things are.

(Mrs. Lynch leaves. O'Malley to the audience.)

O'MALLEY

This is how it started. This is what the LORD says: "A voice is heard in Ramah, mourning and great weeping, Rachel weeping for her children and refusing to be comforted, because they are no more." If hell has no fury like a woman scorned, then beware a grieving and wounded mother, even a life-long Catholic. I felt bad; but had to follow the rules. I was quite sure this was NOT the last time we were going to hear from Mrs. Patrick Lynch.

(BLACK OUT)

(END OF SCENE)

ACT ONE

SCENE 2

SETTING: Office of Sylvia Rappaport DA Investigator. A functional looking bureaucrat's office with metal desk, chairs and file cabinets.

AT RISE: Sylvia Rappaport, 30's, attractive and in a suit is standing near her desk. Mrs. Lynch is seated with a notebook/journal on her lap.

RAPPAPORT

Why did you come to us, Mrs. Lynch?

MRS. LYNCH

I didn't know where to go but knew I wouldn't get anywhere with the diocese and Bishop Bergeron.

RAPPAPORT

What do you mean?

MRS. LYNCH

I'm sure you read or saw something about the death of my son.

RAPPAPORT

That was some time ago. And I remember your protest with the Catholic Church about his burial.

MRS. LYNCH

Ms. Rappaport, I think there was some sinister reason why Eddie took his own life. And toward the end he seemed unhappy and depressed and I think this might explain why.

(Takes notebook/journal off her lap)

RAPPAPORT

What do you mean?

MRS. LYNCH

It took me a while to go through my son's room. When I did, I found this. (Shows Sylvia a notebook/journal; opens and reads) "He would lean against me on his car and mark me with his kisses. I stood frozen. He kissed me and ask if he could bring me to the rectory. I did not want to disrespect him. He was my priest, but I was afraid. He whispered in my ear. I will love you and touch you. You are my very special boy. He would lie on top of me, saying it was normal and okay. And I wondered is this my fault? I was twelve. I was afraid to go to confession." This a restrained part of Eddie's diary. Most of it is much worse, Ms. Rappaport.

RAPPAPORT

Why bring this to us?

MRS. LYNCH

Because I want you to prosecute the beast who drove my son to kill himself. Because I think the Church is protecting him and have no hope that they will do anything about it!

RAPPAPORT

Unless there has been a crime, we have no authority to begin an investigation.

MRS. LYNCH

You mean sexually assaulting children isn't a crime?!

Read the diary. My son was a tortured soul who
~~could not face life because of what that priest had~~
done to him.

RAPPAPORT

The journal doesn't prove anything.

MRS. LYNCH

Then why would he write about the things that
Murtaugh did to him?

RAPPAPORT

How well did you know your son, Mrs. Lynch?

MRS. LYNCH

A mother knows her child. Eddie was a good boy.
His father died when he was a baby. He was never
any trouble; a good student and played football. He
always talked about becoming a doctor.

RAPPAPORT

What about his friends? Drugs? Drinking?

MRS. LYNCH

No, none of that. A few friends.

RAPPAPORT

How about girls?

MRS. LYNCH

Again, he hung around with some, but nothing "serious."

RAPPAPORT

No sad or unhappy love affairs?

MRS. LYNCH

I doubt it. He was a sensitive quiet young man who wanted to help people.

RAPPAPORT

But you said before his suicide he was different.

MRS. LYNCH

He was quiet, withdrawn. Something was bothering

him. He spent a lot of time in his room and wasn't

~~hanging around with his buddies.~~

RAPPAPORT

Are you SURE about the drug thing?

MRS. LYNCH

Look! I knew my son! He was not using any drugs. I know something was troubling him. When I suggested that he go talk to that priest Murtaugh at the parish, he blew up and said some vile things. Eddie had never raised his voice at me. Now I know why.

RAPPAPORT

Mrs. Lynch, you had no idea about these incidents before reading the diary?

MRS. LYNCH

Why would I ever imagine such horrible and repulsive things?

RAPPAPORT

What about your son's suicide? Did you see any signs?

MRS. LYNCH

I would ask him if something was wrong, and he'd say "Nothing to worry about, Mom. I'm going to take care of it." That Sunday he told me to go ahead to Mass. He came in late, then started shouting at Murtaugh, calling him, 'beast, liar, hypocrite and some other awful things. Then he shot himself. I held him until the ambulance came, but I knew he was dead.

RAPPAPORT

And you think that you son's suicide somehow involves this priest because of what you read in his diary?

MRS. LYNCH

Of course, I do!

RAPPAPORT

And what do you want us to do?

MRS. LYNCH

Read the diary. Investigate these crimes and bring this priest to justice!

RAPPAPORT

These crimes are based on entries in a young man's journal. If these are facts, they are serious allegations against the priest. Have you talked to him?

MRS. LYNCH

"Father" Murtaugh has refused to speak to me since he denied Eddie a Christian burial. And I've stopped going to church.

RAPPAPORT

Then Murtaugh's superior. His boss.

MRS. LYNCH

The bishop, Robert Bergeron. He says he has nothing to say to me and he too has refused to see me. I've gone to his office but have been told to leave.

RAPPAPORT

Mrs. Lynch, revelations and allegations about clergy sexual abuse of minors are surfacing all over the country, but investigating the Roman Catholic Church is tricky business.

MRS. LYNCH

Ms. Rappaport, this priest took my son's life long before Eddie's death. He robbed my child's innocence. He mutilated and corrupted my boy. He wounded his soul. I just want him to admit it and the church to stop protecting him

(BLACK OUT)

(END OF SCENE)

SCENE 3

SETTING: The bishop's Office.

AT RISE: Ms. Sylvia Rappaport and the bishop. Rappaport is in her 30's attractive and professionally dressed. She is carrying a briefcase. Bergeron is standing; greets Rappaport then goes to sit behind his desk.

BISHOP

Ms. Rappaport have a seat. Now, what is so important that my secretary said I **had** to see you?

RAPPAPORT

You remember the Eddie Lynch case?

BISHOP

Of course, I do. The mother went to the media because we had to refuse her son burial rites. And, of

18

course, we came off looking cruel, heartless and unforgiving.

RAPPAPORT

So, the news seemed to picture the Church.

BISHOP

As we explained, we could not allow the young man a Catholic funeral because of canon law prohibitions.

RAPPAPORT

Well, it seems that Mrs. Lynch has discovered young Eddie's journal, and there may be more to the story. She came to us with this notebook. (Gets a notebook from her briefcase and hands it to Bergeron)

BISHOP

And what has this got to do with the Catholic Church and me?

RAPPAPORT

The diary alleges that over the course of years young Eddie was sexually assaulted by one of your priests,

a Father Murtaugh. It details sex acts performed by
the priest and names him.

(Bergeron pages through the notebook)

BISHOP

This is pornographic trash! Nonsense! The kid was
mentally unbalanced and took his own life at a Mass
after shouting obscenities and blasphemies at the
priest at the altar for God's sake. This is utter nonsense
and a fabrication! (Puts notebook down on desk)

RAPPAPORT

Well, his mother seems to think that this is what was so
troubling to him and maybe, the reason for what he did.

BISHOP

What does she want? Money. Does she want to
bring this to the reporters and TV? We have attorneys who will fight this.

RAPPAPORT

Bishop Bergeron, I'm not a lawyer. Didn't your secretary tell you, I'm an investigator with the states

attorney's office. We are starting an inquiry and came to you to see if you could provide any information about this priest, Murtaugh. We also have a copy of a letter to you from a Denis Frank in which he too names this priest as a "sexual pervert."

BISHOP

Ms. Rappaport, I'm afraid that any documents or information about our clergy are private and confidential.

RAPPAPORT

And with all due respect…. (Cut off by bishop)

BISHOP

Why are you doing this? You're not a Catholic, are you?

RAPPAPORT

To the first question: Because Eddie and Denis Frank were minors and the fact that we have received a copy of a letter addressed to you that names the same priest makes this suspicious, possibly criminal. And to the second: Does that have any bearing in this inquiry? But just so you know. I'm Jewish.

BISHOP

Then you should know about hateful inuendo and religious persecution.

RAPPAPORT

Yes, as a matter of fact I do. My relatives were from a village in Poland where Jews were massacred even before Hitler. It seems one Sunday the village priest incited some of his parish to take revenge on the "Christ killing Jews" who lived there.

BISHOP

We've asked for forgiveness from the sins of the past, Ms. Rappaport. But what you call an "inquiry," sound like an investigation to me.

RAPPAPORT

Call it what you like Bishop Bergeron. We just want to know if there is any reason to follow up and are asking for your cooperation. Have there been other allegations about this priest to warrant investigation?

BISHOP

Ms. Rappaport, my job, indeed my duty, is to protect the good name of our priests and God's Holy Church.

RAPPAPORT

Then God will give us permission to see any files or information?

BISHOP

Sorry to disappoint you but all records, files and documents in the diocese unfortunately are closed to you.

RAPPAPORT

It seems strange that if you have nothing to hide you would be more willing to see justice done.

BISHOP

This notebook... looks like the sick sexual fantasy of a troubled adolescent. I am sure that none of our clergy would ever intentionally harm a child; much less do anything that involved immorality or violation of celibacy.

RAPPAPORT

Priests are human beings just like anybody. And this notebook seems to imply that at least one of them is a predatory child molester.

BISHOP

(Angrily) You come here with a wild accusation based on a dead boy's diary and expect me to give credence to your suspicions? I think we're finished, Ms. Rappaport. I suggest that you put your allegations in writing. But please know that I will be in touch with our attorneys. (Buzzes for O'Malley, who enters.) I think this lady is leaving.

RAPPAPORT

Thank you for your time, *and* if you don't mind... (Walks to desk and picks up notebook) This is our property and technically, evidence. (Exits with O'Malley)

BISHOP

Michael! Get me Paul Murtaugh's personnel file, now! And call our lawyers and tell them I'm coming to see them.

(Lights fade on Bishop's office.)

O'MALLEY:

(To audience)

Bishop Bergeron really didn't need the file. He knew there had been other complaints. And either out or respect or fear, people had been paid or blackmailed to "keep silent for the good of the Church" about what was called "inappropriate clerical behavior." And sitting on his desk was a letter from a young man named Denis Frank who had been told by his therapist to write to the bishop about his experiences with Father Paul Murtaugh.

(BLACK OUT)

(END OF SCENE)

ACT ONE

SCENE 4

SETTING: Offices of Fairchild and Ashcroft

A well-appointed legal office. Desk and leather chairs. A bar is part of the furnishing.

AT RISE: Walter Ashcroft is seated, as is Bishop Bergeron. Patrick Fairchild is at a bar pouring drink.

FAIRCHILD

Drink, your Excellency? (handing drink to Bergeron)

BISHOP

You know why I'm here? An investigator with the DA came to see me. She has a diary from that psycho kid who killed himself, with details about what Murtaugh did to him. His mother blames us for his suicide. And now this Denis Frank has sent his account of sexual abuse to the media. Says his therapist said it would be good to uncover these wounds

and confront his abuser. It looks like all hell is abd
to break lose.

FAIRCHILD

I've seen that therapist on TV advocating for s
called "hopeless and silent victims" of sexual abus

BISHOP

Ah yes! My old seminary classmate, Dr. Gordd
Wadhams, a media celebrity advocating transpa
ency and openness in the Church admitting there
a serious problem. He doesn't know what a horne
nests he's messing with.

ASHCROFT

Does this Frank have a lawyer? These kinds of sto
ries are surfacing all over and litigation lawyers are
more than happy to relieve the Church of money
"on behalf of their clients."

BISHOP

I don't want to throw money at this, I want you to han
dle it. Keep the lid on it and "talk" to this Denis Frank.

FAIRCHILD

We are lawyers, not magicians. We can't make things disappear.

ASHCROFT

And 'corporate lawyers' at that. This "inquisition" kind of thing is new to us.

BISHOP

Don't quip with me, Ashcroft. Let me remind you, I AM the corporation and I pay you to protect my interest and keep the Church above suspicion.

FAIRCHILD

So, what do you want us to do? Be your spokesman? Deny everything? Seek a settlement with the kids mother and this other person?

ASHCROFT

My first question: Is there anything to these complaints? What kind of history does this alleged perpetrator have?

FAIRCHILD

If we are going to protect you and the Church, what kind of documents exists? Letters, evidence the DA may want to subpoena.

BISHOP

We wouldn't be able to call ourselves "Roman" if we didn't save, copy and document everything. (Factiously)Remember we have the nails from the crucifixion and the crown of thorns. But aren't our files, church property and confidential and privileged?

FAIRCHILD

I don't know? If they are hiding crimes, and I don't know about the statute of limitation. There might well be a lot of legal issues here?

ASHCROFT

Can individual criminal acts become institutionalized? We have a can of worms here!

BISHOP

All I want you to do is protect the good name of the Church. Do whatever it takes, but I will not be bla ⟶ailed by an old lady and a kid into blame and barn ⟶ptcy!

ASHCROFT

First bishop, you do not meet or talk with this Denis Fran let us handle that.

FAIRCHILD

Do n't make any statement or apologize about either case because right now we don't know if these will turn out to be civil or criminal investigations. No comment and silence all around. If you have to make a statement, we will draft it.

ASHCROFT

All the DA has is the diary of and un-hinged kid and the letter of another about this priest. Not much for credible testimony.

FAIRCHILD

Now, about any documents. There can be no collu-sion or cover-up if there is no evidence. Get rid of everything.

ASHCROFT

And just so I know. This Father Murtaugh, are any of the things people are accusing him of, true?

BISHOP

I told you, he's been accused and in trouble before. There's a pattern with young boys, but in the past, we were able to hush it up and the law wasn't involved. Just remember, gentlemen. I want nothing but clear blue sky between the Church and this mess.

ASHCROFT

Like you said, Fear of God" and money, work.

(BLACKOUT)

(END OF SCENE)

ACT ONE

SCENE 5

SETTING: Offices of Fairchild and Ashcroft conference room or legal library. A conference table with chairs

AT RISE: A young man, Denis Frank, mid 20's sits at a conference table. Long hair, kind of ragged looking, nervous; maybe smoking. The lawyers Ashcroft and Fairchild in suits. Fairchild is seated. Ashcroft is standing with a letter of several pages in his hand.

ASHCROFT

Denis, do you know why you're here? It's about this letter. (Holding a letter in his hand.) Bishop Bergeron asked us to talk with you. Tell me about it.

DENIS

Look, I'm not looking for any trouble with lawyers. I wrote the bishop to tell him about Murtaugh and let him know what he'd done to me. Like I said, he told me to trust him and said this was the way boys became men.

FAIRCHILD

If you didn't like all the attention why did you go back?

DENIS

I was a kid. He was my priest. What was I supposed to do? He said he wouldn't be my special friend and I couldn't tell anybody.

FAIRCHILD

So, why did you tell now? Why this letter to Bishop Bergeron?

DENIS

My sister told me she's heard some rumors. And because I am beginning to think it wasn't just me. Once, in grade school I had a fight with Eddie Lynch, and he started shouting that **he** was Murtaugh's "very special friend," and I figure Fr. Murtaugh was doing the same thing to Eddie.

ASHCROFT

Are you telling me you didn't like it? Or that you didn't feel it wasn't right!

DENIS

I was 10 years old! He was my priest!

FAIRCHILD

Calm down, Denis. Where did you meet with Father Murtaugh?

DENIS:

After I served Mass, he would take me to the rectory.

FAIRCHILD

And what would he do?

DENIS

It's all in the letter, do I have to repeat it again?

ASHCROFT

Then why have you waited this long to tell anyone about it? What do you want?

FAIRCHILD

You know the diocese has authorized us to make some sort of settlement.

DENIS

Look, I've spent 14 years dealing with this. Do think any amount of money will change things.

ASHCROFT

We would never suggest that, but what we would like to know is why you sent the bishop this letter and exposed this now.

DENIS

I told you, my sister told me that some parents had complained about Father Murtaugh, and I wanted to help stop the bastard who raped me! She said people are beginning to wonder if their children are safe in parishes and schools and it doesn't seem like the Church is taking any of these allegations seriously.

FAIRCHILD

Why didn't you tell somebody then? Your mom or dad?

DENIS

You think I was going to tell two people who never missed Mass or a novena, said the rosary every night; who had a daughter in the convent, and believed everything **he** told them, that I was being fucked by their priest!!

FAIRCHILD

I know this is very unsettling for you, Denis. But we just want to get some perspective. Tell me, what do you do… for work or a job?

DENIS

I work in a warehouse.

FAIRCHILD

Isn't it true that you've had several jobs and can't hold on to one?

DENIS

I admit, I've had some problems.

FAIRCHILD

Problems!? We have police reports of multiple drunk and disorderly complaints!

DENIS

Lots of times I felt like I was in a deep hole and a dark place. Drinking helped me cope. Maybe it got out of hand.

FAIRCHILD

Let's call it alcoholism. Let's call it a self-inflicted wound.

DENIS

You have no idea what my life has been like!

ASHCROFT

Alright! Let's get off that. In your letter you mentioned your friend Eddie, have you talked to him? Why hasn't he come forward?

DENIS

Because Eddie Lynch blew his brains out. I think he was too sensitive and couldn't live with guilt and shame anymore. And you know that son of a bitch Murtaugh refused to bury him because he'd committed suicide!

ASHCROFT

I want to talk about this letter. You said you were sending a copy to a Sylvia Rappaport; do you know who she is.

DENIS

My therapist said she was some kind of detective investigating these things about kids.

ASHCROFT

So, you told your therapist about this letter too?

DENIS

He said getting it out on paper might help and said I should send it to the bishop, because he was in charge of Murtaugh.

FAIRCHILD

Denis isn't it true that you have been in alcoholic rehab twice in the past.

DENIS

Yes, I admit I have a problem. But what's that got to do with anything we've been talking about? I told a group in rehab once that I started drinking because I thought it would wash away memories of bad things that happened when I was a kid. Some said they understood.

ASHCROFT

What exactly did they 'understand?'

DENIS

Look, I drank to cope with the feeling of shame and anger, and the empty darkness inside me. Alcohol took away all the feeling.

FAIRCHILD

You've been seeing a psychiatrist? Are you having some mental problems?

DENIS

Why? What the hell is this all about?

FAIRCHILD

It's a simple question. Are you being treated for some mental disorder?

DENIS

In the first place, its none of your business! And in the second place I still have nightmares about that bastard, Murtaugh and what he did to me! He stole my childhood and I don't get it back...

ASHCROFT

And you see someone?

DENIS

Yeh... I see someone who is helping me deal with... Are we finished here?

ASHCROFT

Look Denis, we want to believe you, but what you are claiming happened years ago. It's just a little suspicious that you "remembered" all if this, just now when you realized that the Church might be willing to help, financially?

DENIS

I'm not asking for anything. I've just been carrying these memories along with me and I needed to tell someone. The doctor says it's repressed traumatic experience. You don't know what it's like.

FAIRCHILD

Denis, you do realize that it's your word against that of an ordained priest? And that you are **now** just coming forward to tell anybody about what happened?

DENIS

Are you telling me there is a statute of limitations on child rape? He told me then that's what people would say: "No one will believe you." My word against the holy priest! I wrote to the bishop because he's in charge of the son-of-a bitch, and this is how he deals with it? And so, the slaughter of the innocents continues! What do they want? Absolution? Well forget it! I don't care what you say, or they claim. I know what that bastard did to me.

(BLACKOUT)

(END OF SCENE)

ACT ONE

SCENE 6

SETTING: The bishop's office

AT RISE: Bishop at desk. O'Malley with a pack of letters speaks the audience, then goes to bishop's office.

O'MALLEY

Denis Frank kept calling the bishop. He did take a call once and told Denis that he had wounded the Body of Christ with his stories and that he should do penance and seek forgiveness. But after that Bergeron refused to talk to him.

(Full on Bishop's office and O'Malley)

BISHOP

I want these files destroyed especially the letter from this Denis Frank. Shred them, burn them, I don't want any evidence that these complaints reached me. Understand?

O'MALLEY

What if their stories are true?

BISHOP

I don't care if they are. All they want is money. And I'll do anything to keep their hands off it. And get Murtaugh out of that parish. Today!

O'MALLEY

Do you think he's guilty? Do you want me to call him in? Shouldn't we at least investigate these allegations?

BISHOP

Oh, get over it O'Malley. Most of us have been touched, groped, or given the come on by some horny old bastard and our virginity wasn't defiled.

O'MALLEY

But isn't this about innocent, defenseless children?

BISHOP

This isn't about the bad behavior of a priest. It's

about how we protect the Church from scandal and loyalty to the priesthood. So, no statements. No press. Keep this under wraps at all costs. And no paper trail. Deny all claims. Tell the faithful that they have besmirched the priesthood and blackened the name of the holy Church with ugly accusations. Throw in some words like slander and libel. Our lawyers have already discredited this Denis character as a delusional drunk looking for money and publicity.

O'MALLEY

Bishop, this is wrong! Don't these people deserve to be heard? Even Fr. Murtaugh.

BISHOP

Michael. I chose you for this job because you're bright and have promise and are committed to the Church. Michael, we live in broken world, filled with broken people.

O'MALLEY

And aren't we supposed to help them? Do you know what you are doing, bishop? I may be young; but I know right from wrong. And are you trying to bribe me to do something to cover up something that should be investigated? You just **can't pretend** this is not a problem.

BISHOP

Did you hear what I said, O'Malley? I not asking. I'm telling you! You, of all people should understand my position. I am appointed to protect the Church and its priests. I have that burden and responsibility. I am, 'by the grace of God,' shepherd of these people. And I know how to handle this.

O'MALLEY

Haven't these accusations surfaced before? Even before, with Bishop Mancini? Do you really think that burning documents and getting rid of Murtaugh is going to help anybody?

BISHOP

Mancini dealt with these things in his way. I will handle them in mine. Now, call Fred Hopkins and tell him I want to talk to him about getting a new priest in his diocese. Then call Murtaugh and tell him to pack his bags and get out of my diocese. Then get hold of Walter Ashcroft and tell him in need to talk to him immediately.

O'MALLEY

(Apologetically) I mean no disrespect...but you're asking me to be complicit in so many...I can't even think of the word...violations of canon law...and maybe even crimes.

BISHOP

Michael, do you love the Church?

O'MALLEY

That's why I became a priest; to serve the Church and help people do the right thing.

BISHOP

And would you ever want to do anything that would drive people away from the Church? We have to protect her and the people from scandal.

O'MALLEY

Isn't that the job of the Holy Spirit? The real Church exists because of the people.

BISHOP

And I am one of its ordained agents, and this is the way **we** are going to do it. The Church is God's instrument, Michael, even if those who serve it fall short.

O'MALLEY

But it seems so much of this is just... wrong. And the reality is we are trying to pay people for the damage done to them; hiring lawyers to silence and threaten people; and maybe allowing sick or twisted behavior to be hidden and continue. This isn't just about loyalty to the Church. People's lives and priests who may have harmed children are involved.

BISHOP

You're absolutely right, Fr. O'Malley. For right now, for you, it's a question of obedience to authority. My authority. And I have given you direct orders. Now start that process, without your moralizing.

(O'Malley leaves bishops' office.)

O'MALLEY

I had vowed obedience to my bishop at ordination, but that day I didn't want to be part of that Church. I had to face who I was as a human being. Was I just part of an institution that would do anything just to protect itself from scandal? I had to start peeling away my clerical protective layers, that said this was good for the Church and connect with the story of who I thought I was; to see who I *really* was.

(BLACKOUT)

(End OF ACT ONE)

ACT TWO

SCENE 1

SETTINGS: Offices of Ashcroft and Fairchild as before.

AT RISE: Office dark; but spot on O'Malley.

O'MALLEY

Denis Franks' contact with the media and Gordon Wadhams' advocacy opened the floodgates of unreported and secret stories of clergy of sexual abuse that went back decades. Bergeron called on Fairchild and Ashcroft again to quiet the bad publicity. (Fade on O'Malley come up on Office of Ashcroft and Fairchild)

ASHCROFT

Pat, this thing with the diocese is becoming a nightmare. I think we're in over our heads. (Fixes drink) Its more than a public relations problem. It's a disaster!   .

FAIRCHILD

It would appear, my friend, that this is a bit more complicated than an incident with this Father Paul Murtaugh

ASHCROFT:

But it seems that the Church is capable of exorcising ghosts and demons in its own way; with intimidation and if necessary, money.

FAIRCHILD

But our little "interview" with young Mr. Frank, seems to have worked He didn't seem to want his life examined, and in the end, it would be his word against the priest.

ASHCROFT

Case closed, and so far, the district attorney hasn't filed any charges.

FAIRCHILD

The Catholic Church isn't something you take on without absolute evidence. Its seen kingdoms and empires fall and been the victor. And I trust Bishop

Bergeron has destroyed any confirmation and testimony about these allegations.

ASHCROFT

So now what do we do? We can't do miracles and make all this disappear like he expects us to. Don't you think after what he told us about the Church hiding things in the past and his admission that this Murtaugh has a "problem with boys" says something about guilt?

FAIRCHILD

Innocent until proven so, and the Church acted without any criminal intent. And so, Walter, we act like lawyers in defense of our client. Contrary to our advice to remain silent and deny the accusations against Father Murtaugh, we go on the defensive and prepare a public statement for Bishop Robert Bergeron.

ASHCROFT

You mean tell the truth?

FAIRCHILD

Walter, when did you grow a conscience? I mean we make the Church and Bergeron look good, and those accusing the Church of wrongdoing, as misguided and possibly confused and mistaken. We act like lawyers.

ASHCROFT

And how do you propose we do that? By lying?

FAIRCHILD

Let's call it "deceptive truth." Bergeron has already told us about the underhanded way this has been dealt with in the past, we just need to give it a new spin. And it is a good tactic to be simple and direct. I think "God" and "Greed" should fit the bill.

ASHCROFT

What would be the appeal given the media and news coverage?

FAIRCHILD

What about: The Catholic Church is a large institution, but the local church can be subject to apparent misconduct for which it is not accountable. Even though people expect a higher moral standard, its power over conduct is limited. And unscrupulous lawyers see the Church as a money tree to be shaken.

ASHCROFT

Sounds too theoretical. I think we need to focus on the personal.

FAIRCHILD

Okay. We make it personal. The bishop is saddened by the accusations of alleged misconduct of one of his clergy. Dealing with the tragic suicide of her son, a guilt-ridden mother has attacked the Church with a questionable document that implicates the Church. And a publicity seeker has come forward to accuse a priest of sexual abuse that he now recalls, years later, possibly for financial gain? How does that sound?

ASHCROFT

We can't forget this Dr. Wadhams. He is the one that is keeping the pressure on saying there are more and more "victims" and the Church is doing its best to avoid scandal.

FAIRCHILD

I don't think he's a threat. He may be a do-gooder that the media has latched on to. Soon this will become old news. The "cloak of religion" will protect the Church. There's no reason to panic Walter. If Wadhams keeps pushing his agenda, even an institution like the Church, will become a "victim."

ASHCROFT

And you think that a statement by the bishop will help?

FAIRCHILD

Never let anyone like Wadhams score points and be caught without a counter solution. I think it's time Bishop Bergeron makes a public statement; we might even suggest a private meeting with Dr. Wadhams. If we do this right, we should look for a bonus from the diocese.

ASHCROFT

Is it possible for all this to backfire? Don't you think this strategy is risky?

FAIRCHILD

Bishop Bergeron came to us for advice. He has priests and other advisors. He wants us to smother this. This is what you and I are suggesting as his legal counsel; all private, all confidential.

ASHCROFT

And a good principle would be: Never tell anybody more than necessary.

FAIRCHILD

Then all we have to do is draft a statement; call the bishop and see if we can arrange a press conference. Do you want to call his office?

(BLACKOUT)

(END OF SCENE

ACT TWO

SCENE 2

SETTING: The Bishop's Office

AT RISE: Bishop Bergeron at desk. O'Malley enters with a bunch of letters. Goes to put them on Bergeron's desk.

O'MALLEY

I found these letters in going through the files.

BISHOP

Damn it, Michael, I've told you to destroy any letter with these filthy allegations. I've been advised not to respond to them. But put them on the desk.

O'MALLEY

These are old letters. Some going back before Bishop Mancini. You may want to look at them. You've seen the people outside. Some of their signs say: "Evil thrives here." And there are things that are being found out all over the country about priests in other dioceses. You just can't ignore that something isn't going on here. Even some of the priests are beginning to wonder.

BISHOP

Wonder about what?

O'MALLEY

Assignments that are moving priests overnight. Priests being sent away with no explanation. Paying people for silence – or as you say for the "good of the diocese."

BISHOP

You, Father O'Malley are here to do as I say. Because in this corner of God's earth, I am Christ's vicar, his voice. And what I say goes, is that understood.

O'MALLEY

Yes, bishop. I'll just leave these on your desk.

(O'Malley exits. Bergeron glances at the stack of letters, then picks one up. The voices of the victims are heard. Bergeron then reads his response and discards or tears up the letter.)

WOMAN'S VOICE

I was just 14 when I had sex with him. When he found out I was pregnant, he said I had to get an abortion. How could a priest tell me that? And now they tell me that that abortion was so botched that I can never have children. What are you doing about this?

BISHOP

(Reading from his response) Father has been sent to a monastery for a period of prayer and reflection and I hope that you have sought the sacrament of penance for the grave sin of abortion.

MAN'S VOICE

When we were on a retreat he crept into my bed at night and made me touch him. Why do you let him be around young kids?

BISHOP

We have moved this priest to an assignment where he is not in contact with teenage boys.

WOMAN'S VOICE

I was alone with him after a basketball game in the parish gym. He pressed himself against me and fondled my breasts. None of my teachers believed me and laughed when I told them it was my priest. I hear that this has happened to other girls.

BISHOP

Father has been sent for psychological evaluation.

MAN'S VOICE

In the rectory, he took me and my little brother upstairs. Then he told us to take off all our clothes and get on the bed. He took pictures of us and before we left gave us crosses because we were "good boys." Why would no one believe us? And why is this guy still a priest?

BISHOP

We truly regret the incident you describe. We are in the middle if a capital campaign and funds are limited. However, we are prepared to provide settlement in the following amount should you be willing to sign a nondisclosure agreement.

WOMAN'S VOICE

He said if I didn't do it, I couldn't be in the choir any-more. He would come to my house when my parents weren't home and force me to have sex with him. Once he slapped me. I was afraid to tell anybody. But now I'm writing to you because you are in charge of these priests.

BISHOP

I regret to inform you that the priest in question has retired and is now living in Florida.

WOMAN'S VOICE

My 12-year-old son was an altar boy and idolized priests. Last week he hanged himself. I think I know why my darling son didn't want to live. Our priest used to invite him to spend the night in the priest's house. Then he would give him alcohol and when he was drunk would have sex with him. I know this now because at my son's funeral some parents came and said that he had been accused of the same thing in another parish. They said you keep moving this monster from parish to parish. How in God's name can you permit this pervert...

BISHOP

Rumors of this sort are very detrimental, none of these accusations have ever been substantiated. And the priest in question has been reassigned for pastoral reasons.

MAN'S VOICE

He told me that because priests couldn't marry this is the way they had sex. Who was I going to ask? Another priest? I was 11 years old and without a father. How was I to know? Weren't they supposed to speak for God?

BISHOP

Tell your attorney at we are prepared to settle this allegation of sexual impropriety outside of litigation.

WOMAN'S VOICE

My mom would cook dinner for him and make me take it to the rectory. He would always come to the door in his bathrobe and expose himself. He told me that anal sex was not fornication. The bastard gave me a venereal disease when I was 14. Why is no one listening to us?

BISHOP

Your letter to the Apostolic Nuncio has been forwarded to me. We regret any pain and suffering from these alleged incidents, but your repeated threats about going to the media amount to blackmail and will not be tolerated. I informed you that this matter was closed with the death of the priest in question. Any attempt to vilify the diocese will be met with appropriate legal action or canonical penalties.

BISHOP

(Calls for O'Malley.) O' Malley come in here. And bring my calendar (O' Malley enters) (Bergeron hands O'Malley the torn letters) Take all this trash and burn it. Now, what's my calendar look like? Isn't my seminary class reunion coming up? Judge Fenton called me and told me to look for a formal invite; said that I shouldn't miss this one. Something special. I haven't seen what's left of those guys in years.

O'MALLEY

The judge told me that some of your class is trying to hold it at the old seminary. They say that its sold, and they wanted to ramble around its sacred halls before the developer gets a hold of it. They think the old place is going to be torn down. (Hands Bishop calendar.)

BISHOP

Call Ed Dempsey and tell him I can join a foursome for golf Friday morning. Have Confirmation at St. Ann's in the evening. And tell that head doctor Wadhams that I'll see him. Maybe it's about our seminary reunion.

(Lights fade. A single spot on what looks like a confessional with a priest in cassock and stole sitting in the center.)

PRIEST

The dark box where banal sins are told by frightened little girls. I tell them to sit in Father's lap. I can smell the baby powder on them. I can smooth their hair as they squirm across my lap. So pure and innocent as I touch them and tell them not to squirm. But I'm not worried. I know the Church will watch out for me and defend the priesthood.

(BLACK OUT)

(END OF SCENE)

ACT TWO

SCENE 3

SETTING: Bishop Bergeron on stage at a podium with crest of the Diocese of Ste. Pierre on the front. The bishop's motto: 'Ecclesiam Defende' is part of the crest. A large crucifix behind him.

AT RISE: Bishop Bergeron alone at podium.

BISHOP

I want to thank the members of the press and media for coming. I will not be taking questions, but on the advice of our attorneys I will be making a statement about the allegations of clergy misconduct in the Diocese of Ste. Pierre.

We have been silent amid these accusations, a victim of vicious and scandalous attacks against the Holy Church and its priests; rumors and gossip without credible evidence or witnesses.

The pain of the past few months has torn at the heart of the Church.

First, there was the tragic death of a young man who took his own life in front of a church filled with worshippers. For us, a sacrilegious desecration of a consecrated place.

His grieving and guilt-ridden mother seeking answers for his death says she found proof that his self-destructive despair was the result of years of sexual abuse by one of our priests.

Recently another young man, at the instigation of his psychiatrist or psychotherapist, has "recalled" "similar" abuse as a child. He now has come forward to tell or "sell" his story to the media.

For me and the people of the Diocese of Ste. Pierre, these are painful episodes in the life of our local church. And let me assure you that there has not been any mismanagement or deception on our part as some have suggested. The integrity and sanctity of the good name of the Church has been our chief concern.

Civil authorities have been unable to find any credible evidence for these accusations and complaints.

At the center of this controversy is a priest of this diocese, Father Paul Murtaugh, who has served the people of this diocese for many years.

It is with profound distress that I have to announce

the Father Murtaugh, the priest named in these slanderous claims, is seeking service in another diocese. He makes this decision with regret, but due to the destructive publicity and even threats against his life, finds it impossible to perform his priestly duties in a climate of suspicion and fear.

Personally, I have been appalled by the demonstrations and protest at his parish and at the offices of the diocese. They insinuate a climate of cover-up and collusion, but nothing could be further from the true intention of the Church.

My hope and prayer are that this sad and unfortunate chapter has been closed. I beg those involved to seek forgiveness for the damage done to the name of the Church and her priests and in a spirit of reconciliation pray that they may find peace.

I also pray that I can now, once again, focus on the work entrusted to me as shepherd of the faithful in this part of God's kingdom.

Again, Thank you all. (Walks off)

(BLACKOUT)

(END OF SCENE)

ACT TWO

SCENE 4

SETTING: The Office of Sylvia Rappaport, as before.

AT RISE: Mrs. Lynch is pacing, agitated.

Rappaport is seated at her desk.

MRS. LYNCH

I can't believe the deceit and arrogance of that man in that press conference! To call this a "malicious scandal." And that malevolent fiend Murtaugh is getting away!

RAPPAPORT

Mrs. Lynch, I told you I went to see Bishop Bergeron and got nowhere.

MRS. LYNCH

You had proof!

RAPPAPORT

I don't want to minimize this, but legally, at this time and in this state, we are dealing with a lot of constraints.

MRS. LYNCH

What do you mean?

RAPPAPORT

People in this office couldn't agree there was any direct evidence for your son's suicide in the journal. Nowhere does he talk about self-destruction, just despair for the whole situation. Then there is a question of **when** did these things take place.

MRS. LYNCH

You mean dates?

RAPPAPORT

No, but there is such a thing as the statute of limitations. It is the maximum time after an event within which legal proceedings may be initiated.

MRS. LYNCH

There's a legal limit on the molesting of my son?

RAPPAPORT

No but under current law victims of sexual battery aged 16 or older must report the crime within 72 hours. And there were no dates in Eddie's accounts, and it seems like some of these encounters happened while Eddie was much younger? Was there no suspicion, no signs?

MRS. LYNCH

My God, I've lost my only son and didn't know why my innocent boy would be so desperate as to take his own life. Why would I think such repulsive and unspeakable things were being done to him?

RAPPAPORT

(Rises and goes to Mrs. Lynch) I can't imagine what you're feeling Mrs. Lynch. Sometimes, grief or guilt make us look for explanations where there are none. (Picks up the diary)One of the people we contacted to assess the diary said that a good lawyer might even suggest it was adolescent fictional fantasy.

MRS. LYNCH

But he names Murtaugh. And, God help me, some of the incidents are so disturbing and graphic I had to stop reading

RAPPAPORT

Exactly. Stuff like this is often dismissed as "false memories." Victims have difficulty recalling specific details and because Eddie's diary was so specific, he might have made things up.

MRS. LYNCH

What about this young man, Denis, who went to the press and wrote to the bishop? Is he making things up too?

RAPPAPORT

I talked with him, after a grilling by the diocesan attorneys. The problem in this kind of case with clergy is their standing in the community. With no evidence to back up any victim's testimony; it's a question of who do you believe.

MRS. LYNCH

You mean he doesn't want to see this monster brought to justice or punished?

RAPPAPORT

It's not that; but the lawyers convinced him that he would be on trial as much as the priest he is accusing. He said he didn't want to face that.

MRS. LYNCH

So, my son is dead; a victim of disbelief, another silenced young man, and the devil that destroyed him is free and gone to corrupt and pervert.

RAPPAPORT

I'm afraid, his move, out of state, puts him outside our jurisdiction. I'm sorry.

MRS. LYNCH

(Quietly and pensively) You know Ms. Rappaport, after all this time, I don't know your name.

RAPPAPORT

Sylvia.

MRS. LYNCH

Sylvia, you're not a mother, are you?

RAPPAPORT

No, but I hope to be some day.

MRS. LYNCH:

Then you will understand a love that lasts forever. Mothers are supposed to protect their children. When I lost Eddie's father, my boy was all I had. When he killed himself, I think before I felt grief, I was angry. Angry at myself because I couldn't save my child, even angry at God. I kept asking: "Why?" And I couldn't come up with an answer. Children shouldn't die before us and Eddie's death was a mystery. You never expect to bury your child but when the Church forbid his funeral, I can't tell you about my pain. Then I found that damn diary! And then I knew I had failed to help him. That he kept a secret that his heart could not hold any longer. And the Church that had refused to acknowledge my son's death was the reason why he killed himself!

RAPPAPORT

Mrs. Lynch, I sympathize with you. Personally, I believe that there was a connection between your son's death and this priest's abuse. I also believe that your bishop, Bergeron, knew something, and he wants to save himself and your Church from embarrassment. But legally there's nothing we can do.

(BLACKOUT)

(END OF SCENE)

ACT THREE

SCENE 1

SETTING: The bishop's and O'Malley's Offices.

AT RISE: O'Malley, at his desk reading, almost praying from the Scripture. Bishop's office dark but Bergeron at desk.

O'MALLEY

But among you there must not be even a hint of sexual immorality, or of any kind of impurity, or of greed, because these are improper for God's holy people. Therefore, let no one deceive you with empty words, for because of these things the wrath of God comes upon the sons of disobedience. Do not be partakers with them; for you were formerly darkness, but now you are Light in the Lord; walk as children of Light (for the fruit of the Light *consists* in all goodness and righteousness and truth), trying to learn what is pleasing to the Lord. Do not participate in the unfruitful of darkness, but instead even expose them; for it is disgraceful even to speak of the things which are done by them in secret. But all things become visible when they are exposed by the light, for everything that becomes visible is light.

(Gordon Wadhams knocks at doorcase, speaks to O'Malley).

GORDY

Gordon Wadhams, here to see, Bishop Bergeron.

O'MALLEY

Yes, Dr. Wadhams. Just one minute. (Goes to bishop's office).

O'MALLEY

Dr. Wadhams is here. He made an appointment. Remember? Said it was important and confidential. I told him you might see him at the seminary reunion.

BISHOP

I know what he wants, and really don't want to talk to him, but send him in. (O'Malley exits. Gordon Wadhams enters and is greeted.)

BISHOP

Dr. Wadhams, it's been ages. How have you been?

GORDY

Fine, your excellency.

BISHOP

The last time I saw you was at our seminary re-union a while back. Have a seat. And let's skip the formality. What brings the good Dr. Wadhams to see me?

GORDY

I'm afraid it's a delicate and confidential matter. You know I'm a therapist. And people come and tell me where they hurt. Hopefully, I try to help them find out why.

BISHOP

Gordon, I've spent decades in the confessional. I know about the dark side of human nature.

GORDY

People sometimes tell me more than they would tell their priest and in the past months I've seen an alarming number of people, who claim they are victims of clergy sexual misconduct or abuse. They tell me they've written or contacted you and gotten a run-a-round.

BISHOP

(Almost angrily) And this "alarming number of people" they've borne their souls without any of your psycho-babble probing no doubt? Tell me, has that Rappaport woman put you up to this? Or that witch Mrs. Lynch?

GORDY

Look, I'm here on my own because people are hurt and dealing with trauma after decades and it seemed to me that you should have some interest in...

BISHOP

(Interrupting) I don't want to sound defensive, Gordon, but you know that I've been dealing with some of these claims. Some of them go back years. We have dealt with isolated incidents and disciplined the priests.

GORDY

But I'm getting the impression that your predecessors ignored, even covered up some very disturbing …

BISHOP

(Again angrily.) Wait a minute! Our investigations have shown that people got lawyers to seek damages against the diocese; that some of their stories were a vicious way of pay-back to a priest for an imagined grievance or romantic fantasy. And finally, most of the allegations are faulty and foggy memories of adults who are now alleging abuse that they never told anyone about when they were children. And because lawyers are involved, money!

GORDY

I'm not sure this is all about money? Some of these people are dealing with trauma after decades. Is there a time limit on the truth, bishop? Simply because something evil happened in the past doesn't make it less evil now.

BISHOP

I think you're over-reacting and might even want to open some Pandora's box based on what you perceive as arrogant negligence. Frankly, that is offensive to me and to the Church.

GORDY

No offense intended, bishop, I came because I still believe, like those days in the seminary, that the Church should always be with those without a voice.

BISHOP

Sometimes, Dr. Wadhams, the Church has to listen to its own voice.

GORDY

But never, I hope, at the cost of losing its decency by deliberately lying.

BISHOP

I can assure you that the Church has, and will always be, faithful.

GORDY

You know that I'm under no sacramental seal of silence and legally obliged to report abuse.

BISHOP

But you do have a duty of confidentiality to your clients who may not want to dredge up the past.

GORDY

I have a duty to protect innocent people from abuse!

BISHOP

Even if this will drive people away from the Church?

GORDY

How can concealing these things help? Hiding the truth by omission is worse than a lie.

BISHOP

Gordy, you came here to share your concerns. Duly noted. Now, I hate to rush you, but I have other appointments. Trust me, everything is being done to ensure the integrity of the Church. Good to see you.

GORDY

(Wadhams rises to go, then stops and turns to bishop.) I get the impression that I am being "handled" and dismissed like some of the people I've talked to. They said they were told that you would "investigate" their stories and take appropriate action. But all you did was hide some very...

BISHOP

(Angrily.) Wait a minute... the Church has always dealt with what you are talking about in the best way it knows how and in the best interest of the Church. That's why we are here.

GORDY

The people who are coming to me are not talking about ecclesiastical concern and compassion. Their experience doesn't match your statements.

BISHOP

Look, I saw you today because I knew you from the time we were both studying for the priesthood and all you want to do is dredge up the past and infer that some long dead priests and bishops covered up sin and perversion.

GORDY

(A little angrily.) I'm telling you, bishop, that I am dealing with wounded survivors whose stories were dismissed, suppressed or covered up. And what's worse, some of their abusers have been allowed to continue to pray on innocent children. You seem to be treating this like some temporary lapse of character that can be excused because of the privilege position of priests! Not deviant behavior!

BISHOP

You have some nerve coming to me with ethical imperatives as if the Church has lost its moral compass. Many of your so called "victims" have had no problem dipping into the pockets of the Church. And many still have difficulty distinguishing what is "good" for the Church.

GORDY

And what might that be?

BISHOP

She doesn't air her dirty laundry in public.

GORDY

But this isn't about Holy Mother the Church's HONOR. It's about her children.

BISHOP

All you righteous types seem to forget free will and guilt.

GORDY

I'm talking about gross assaults made on children by men they were told to trust and obey, who could have told them that up was down and wrong was right!

BISHOP

Are you a good Catholic, Dr. Wadhams?

GORDY

As good as I can be.

BISHOP

Then you can remember when we were confirmed we promised to die rather than dishonor the Church.

"White martyrdom" I think the nuns called it. Well I pledged fidelity to the Church when I was ordained and when I was made a bishop. And that's what I will do.

GORDY

Can't even very good men do the wrong thing for what they think is a greater good?

BISHOP

If what you say is right, then you came here to be a conscience for the Church, and I am running out of ways to tell you that there is no immoral corporate plot to hide anything.

GORDY

I came to you hoping to persuade you to be honest, and above all truthful about your priests who think they are still free to abuse and assault children.

BISHOP

I resent your tone and attitude, Dr. Wadhams. You know Gordy, even in the seminary, I thought you had a 'messiah complex' Perhaps that's why you became a shrink. You enjoy saving people. (Rings for O'Malley.) Father O'Malley will you come in here. (O'Malley comes in.) Father, will you please show Dr. Wadhams out.

GORDY

(Handing Bergeron his card.) My card in case you or anyone who contacts you might be looking for professional clinical help or referral. Anyone. (O'Malley and Wadhams both leave.)

BISHOP

(Calls for O'Malley.) O' Malley come in here. And bring my calendar. (O'Malley enters with calendar.)

O'MALLEY

May I ask? What did he want? He was kind of evasive when he called for an appointment. Said he knew you and he needed to see you personally.

BISHOP

Dr. Wadhams is a troublemaker, Father, and I don't need his advice. I don't want to see him again. Make some excuse if he calls back. (Lights fade on bishop's office)

O'MALLEY

Bishop Bergeron was right. I was young, and naïve. The past year had shown me a side of the Church that was nothing like the one I imagined. After all this was the "new" Church after Vatican II, open, socially conscious. A Church where all were called to holiness by priests and bishops who were to be examples. Rituals and ceremonies that people could understand and take part in. But I was seeing a cold, merciless and manipulative Church that was willing to lie, hide and protect horrendous evil. It was a crisis and I didn't know where these doubts would lead.

(BLACKOUT)

(END OF SCENE)

ACT THREE

SCENE 2

SETTING: The Office of Dr. Gordon Wadhams. Comfortable furniture with a sofa and chairs.

AT RISE: Wadhams and John Fenton, Franco Terranova, Henry Campion, all former seminary classmates of Bishop Bergeron, are seated or standing.

FENTON

Why did you call us?

GORDY

Jack, I wanted to tell you about my meeting with his excellency-holier than thou-Bergeron.

FENTON

Wait a minute. I thought this was about making plans for our seminary class reunion.

HENRY

What's to plan? Some booze and food, then hours of stupid stories and telling each other how well things are going.

GORDY

Jack, I went to see our old classmate, Robert Bergeron about some of my clients, victims of clergy sexual abuse. They tell me they've written or tried to contact him and gotten a run-a-round. I went to see him and got the same dismissive arrogance.

FENTON

So, you went to see him? I still thought this was about making plans for The Boy Bishop Festival on Holy Innocents Day, like the ole days.

GORDY

I suspect our old classmate is involved in some form of collusion and Church scheme to hide its past sin and avoid or ignore the complaints of victims of sexual abuse now. And I'm sure that involves shielding and protecting perpetrators who are priests. And I've tried to see him or talk to him again. His secretary, O'Malley keeps telling me that the bishop's calendar is full and its "confirmation season."

HENRY

Or maybe he's just a busy man trying to run a "multimillion-dollar franchise" called a diocese.

FENTON

Gordy, how is this our problem? Once again, are we to plan a reunion in the old haunts before they tear the rubble down?

GORDY

Don't you think this scandal with priests is serious, Jack?

FENTON

I don't see any point of making a drama out of a Church crisis. You can't do anything because of patient confidentiality and as far as I can tell he's managed to silence or discredit anybody who has come forward. I know for sure that a couple of complaints have been thrown out for lack of credible witness, and the like.

HENRY

And I also know that the diocese has secretly paid hush money with the proviso of non-disclosure. All legal.

GORDY

Legal, but is it moral? You can't use religion to control people!

HENRY

Gordy, I think the "moral" part is Bobby Bergeron's job!

FRANCO

Gordy, we only see him every couple of years for the gabfest we call a "reunion," which is a chance to congratulate each other on how well we are doing and catch up on what's going on in our lives. I've seen the press and read his self-serving 'the Church as victim,' interview.

GORDY

But don't you get the feeling that he's covering up a lot?

HENRY

Bob Bergeron has always acted like he was superior, a pain in the ass. And you know that people have always had tolerance for the peccadillos and fumbling of the Church.

FRANCO

Otherwise it would never have survived. And you know that you have always been a bleeding heart. Compassion, justice, honesty and integrity; you would have made a good priest.

FENTON

Again, I ask. Why is this our problem. I've been a Catholic all my life and know the Church has always had secrets and gone to any length to keep it that way.

GORDY

Jack, I've seen people's lives shattered, families in despair dealing with deep festering wounds of unspoken abuse by people who Bergeron is protecting. As I remember it, we all wanted to help people and do good. That's why we thought we wanted to be priests.

FRANCO

(Slyly) Until we got certain other ideas and urges.

HENRY

Look, we've all been friends for a long time, from those days in the seminary. From time to time we've even helped each other out. Like brothers, but are you suggesting that we take on the Catholic Church? Are you insane? Since when have we been crusaders?

GORDY

Not the whole "Big Momma." Just one cog. Just one of her sons.

FENTON

And you know it's a "mother" who will do mostly anything to protect her priests.

GORDY

And her secrets. I think my patients are just the tip of the iceberg. I've talked to colleagues and, they are treating and listening to just too many people who are dealing with issues related to childhood abuse and their stories more and more involve a member of the Catholic clergy right here. And people are wondering if their children are safe.

HENRY

Remember, we once thought that was where we were headed. We were surrounded by them and never once did I feel that they had any dirty thoughts.

GORDY

Are you that naïve, Henry? Remember the one we called "Moose?" Who always wanted someone to come up to his room "for confession?"

FRANCO

Let's not go down there. Most of us gave up the idea long ago that ordaining people made them saints. I read somewhere that at any given time only about half the priests in the US practice celibacy.

GORDY

I'm not surprised by that. Adults with adults; that's one thing. What I'm telling you about are innocent young kids and deviant behavior and a pattern that's gone on for years. And I know that Bergeron knows it has gone on and is still going on. And he's in the middle of this mess.

FENTON

Okay, Calm yourself, Gordy. I know I haven't seen him since we were at Carry's funeral. And then it was "Hello-can't chat. Pressing business at the chancery. Good to see you."

GORDY

I'd say...Another press conference; answering questions about why certain priests suddenly were no longer in this diocese and seemed to have disappeared altogether.

HENRY

I've seen him on TV. Very dignified; spoke well. Told of his personal pain over the malicious rumors and there is nothing to them. And the whole thing is getting out of hand with death threats to priests. Do you think he's lying?

GORDY

I just know what people are telling me. And when I went to see him; he blew me off with some sanctimonious bullshit that he's handled this in the "best interest of the Church." I think...I know...he's covering up a lot and hiding behind the Church.

FENTON

So, I keep on asking...What are we supposed to do about it? Lawyers? Media? Or join those people picketing outside the chancery saying there is evil inside? I'm a district judge, Henry's on the board of a couple of corporations, and you think we should get involved in this tangle? Franco what do you think?

FRANCO

Well, in the middle ages, clergy were excommunicated, defrocked and degraded for lesser offences. And so far, Robert Bergeron seems to have talked his way out of a scandal swirling around him. I'm not looking to make this a witch hunt, but I think we could talk to him.

HENRY

Or somebody? Maybe the archbishop. A letter a phone call.

GORDY

Do you honestly think that one of their own is going to listen to us who think they have been betrayed by their bishop and he is allowing the continued sexual assault of children!

FENTON

And you think Robert Bergeron is going to tell his old classmates the truth, because we all were in the seminary together? Remember, he's more than a "company man," Here he **is** the "Company."

GORDY

No, what if I can convince some of my patients to come to us and tell us their stories. Most of them only want to be heard so that others won't be harmed because they were silent. Maybe then, we can do something to bring some truth and justice and possibly some peace to these victims and their families.

HENRY

I hate to seem cynical, but I feel like we should be humming some theme music behind you now, Gordy. You are suggesting that we go up against one of the most powerful global organizations on the face of the planet!

GORDY

I only want to deal with one man, who is part of it.

FENTON

This is personal with you, isn't it? A crusade against the "institution."

GORDY

An institution that protects predators and buys silence. An institution that apparently prefers to protect an image than tell the truth. An institution whose motto should be: "Better to look good than to be good." I don't think this is what Jesus intended.

HENRY

Okay, But I hope we know what we're doing? Possibly accusing a prelate of the Roman Catholic Church of lying to cover his ass and providing protection to sexual predators. We'd be opening a can of worms, with possible legal trouble.

FRANCO

Speaking for myself why should I care about any of this. Frankly, I'm not what you might call a "good" Catholic anymore. Too much education, I guess. Christmas and Easter and an occasional funeral or family christening for me. Gordy, what is it you want? Confession? Apology? Bob to admit he's been covering up?

GORDY

All I want **you** to do is hear the stories I've heard. I want you to see the human wreckage of people who were violated by men who said they were God's anointed. I want you to see the tears of mothers and fathers who have nightmares about children who took their own lives because they felt guilty and ashamed. I want Robert Bergeron to admit that he has responsibility for all this.

FRANCO

You do know this is about power and authority and Bergeron will do anything to control it and keep it from public scandal. (A long silence)

GORDY

No matter what we believe, the one thing we all promised each other back then, was that we would always do the right thing. And I think the least we can do is hear these people out who were abused, damaged, raped or molested repeatedly buy men wearing roman collars.

FRANCO

Do you honestly believe that we can do something about this... this sickness that has been going on for centuries? The church has always been complicit and secretive in these types of scandals; they just didn't get publicity like now. This whole discussion is ridiculous.

GORDY

I'm not laboring under any delusion that we can change a lot, but I think we can do something for these powerless people who deserve a voice. People we once said we wanted to serve. Just tell me Franco, when is enough, enough?

FRANCO

All I'm saying is that if "Holy Mother the Church" and the Vatican hasn't done a damn thing to discipline priests or bishops, how on earth do you expect to get Robert Bergeron's attention?

HENRY

What might you suggest? Something like a scarlet letter embroidered on his cassock. Or a sign around his neck with the charge of "criminal collusion."

FRANCO

Or maybe something medieval and dramatic. I can see the headlines: "Pedophile Perpetrators' Protector Does Public Penance."

GORDY

I'm serious, Franco. I don't know, but whatever it will be we'd best be very creative about it.

FENTON

Okay? Are we agreed? (Pause for approval from all present.) Gordy, you supply the people. We'll listen to what they have to say. And then? Who knows? You do know that all of us are really sticking our necks out here. And now can we talk about the reunion in the old seminary before it crumbles by itself?

HENRY

All I remember about those days is the silly and stupid tradition of the "Boy Bishop" on the Feast of the Holy Innocents supposedly slaughtered by Herod. We'd elect a 'bishop' and dress him up and we all had to obey him, no matter what. It was supposed to teach us blind obedience to authority. And there was always wine and a banquet...

(BLACKOUT)

(END OF SCENE)

ACT THREE

SCENE 3

SETTING: A large community room of the semi-nary with large gothic window, set for a reunion reception. A small bar and tall cocktail tables and a few folding chairs scattered over the room.

AT RISE: Bergeron's seminary classmates with the addition of Terry Fowler, are clustered together, some with drinks. There are other "guests" men and women in groups in murmuring conversation. Michael O'Malley forward.

O'MALLEY

I asked Bishop Bergeron to be reassigned to a parish where I was saying Mass on the weekends, but he said that more than ever he needed a secretary who was a priest. And even when I suggested other names, he refused. I told him I was thinking about talking to that investigator Sylvia Rappaport and he went insane, asking me: "Whose side was I on?" And calling me

"Judas" and "Betrayer." And old and wise priest that I had been seeing suggested I petition Rome for a leave of absence due to a mental health crisis involving my vocation. One thing I had as bishop's secretary were the right names and addresses. I have to confess that through all this mess I couldn't pray. I just wondered where God was in all of it, and if he, or she, had taken sides? I eventually was granted lay status.

The day I left the office Bergeron warned me that my soul was in danger if I even thought of betraying the Church. Dr. Wadhams and Judge Fenton had been calling just about every week to tell me it was important to remind the bishop about their class reunion saying he couldn't miss it. They would even send a car to make sure he was there as their very special guest. (Lights on seminary common room)

FENTON

No, of the two dozen or so who started here, only Bob Bergeron and Fred Wright went on to ordination. Most of the guys that came here wanting to be priests have met their Maker.

TERRY

Bergeron did all right, bishop and all that. Faithful Son of Holy Mother.

HENRY

Is Wright still a priest in the Amazon? Anybody know?

FENTON

Must be, got an appeal letter from his mission, for his beloved Indians.

FRANCO

The rest of us didn't do too badly. (Nodding to those around). A judge, a couple of lawyers, university faculty. No medicine men, but some shrinks. I'm surprised so few decided to come to this.

FENTON

I wonder if all of us are still Catholic after all these years. I sent invitations to most I had an address for. We'll have some other guests, and you four got special invites, of course.

GORDY

What about our bigtime bishop? Isn't he here yet?

FENTON

No, but the night won't be the same without him.

(Bishop Bergeron comes in, greets and is greeted by the men present.)

GORDY

Speak of the devil.

FRANCO

Drink, Bob? Your excellency. Some…?

BISHOP

Johnny Walker will do fine. (Franco goes to bar for drink)

TERRY

Probably need it after this week playing to the merciless media over this abuse thing. Seems like its reached critical mass.

BISHOP

We're dealing with the situation. Could we **not** talk

about that tonight? Just some drinking and reminiscing as I recall. (Franco returns and hands drink to bishop.)

TERRY

Tell me Bishop Bob, is it true that there are two things that bishops can never get.

BISHOP

Terry, had to many of those already? As usual you don't know what you're talking about.

TERRY

But I've heard they never get good advice or a bad meal!

(He laughs.)

BISHOP

Always a fool, Terry. I know it's been a long time since the last reunion, but I don't recognize half of these guys.

TERRY

That's what happens after I've had a few drinks myself.

BISHOP

And it seems like there are some women. Have wives been invited? This is new since the last time. Guess that will lessen the bawdy stories and nostalgic memories about our time here.

FENTON

Do you remember when Donohue fell asleep and fell out of his pew and we all thought he was possessed, and we were afraid to go near him.

TERRY

With all we heard about the "dangers" of private – or was it "personal friends," it's a wonder that anybody went to help him. It's almost a miracle we've managed to remain such good friends after all these years!

HENRY

Just the thing we were talking about before you arrived. Remember the Passion Play we put on.

TERRY

I recall that someone, who didn't show up to-night, liked putting on a wig and dressing like Mary Magdalen so much that it became a lifestyle! (Chuckles)

BISHOP

Of course. Triumphal entry. Betrayal by Judas. A Last Supper and, of course, Pilate asking Jesus: "What is Truth?"

FENTON

A great question, huh Bob?

BISHOP

(Almost defensively) What are you suggesting, Fenton?

FENTON

Oh, nothing. Just how difficult it is to find out the truth. Or sometimes, even telling the truth. It's just a judge's kind of question. It's a question we judges face every day.

FRANCO

Remember what happened when the rector caught us in a lie? (In an imperious voice.) "I'm afraid you'll have to spend time in the crypt, young man."

HENRY

I wonder why he thought that would be a place to amend our lying ways? It was creepy down there.

FRANCO

Probably so we would consider the evil our lies had done and the darkness it had brought upon us.

HENRY

Maybe, but I think it was just to scare the hell out of us. I hated the place.

TERRY

I wonder if there are any ghosts of our past sins still down there?

HENRY

I can still smell incense and candle smoke.

FRANCO

As I remember it, most of the smoking took place where we wouldn't get caught.

TERRY

Are you sure it's not the smell of your socks in your gym locker?

FRANCO

Could we act like grown men? We sound like college kids!

BISHOP

I, for one, can say, I never spent any time down there.

FENTON

Then maybe it's time for a visit. What the hell, there's nobody here, let's go down there. Take your drinks.

GORDY

Remember, gentlemen, we shouldn't be afraid of the dark.

(Lights dim as group moves toward an exit.)

(BLACK OUT)

(END OF SCENE)

ACT THREE

SCENE 4

SETTING: The crypt, a large low vaulted room with arches and pillars. Dimly lit with shafts of light.

AT RISE: Out of the shadows a group of men and women encircle Bishop Bergeron. They put a mitre and cope on him. Denis Frank and Mrs. Lynch are among them. They seem to fade away into the darkness. The rest of the reunion group, Fenton, Wadhams, Campion, Terranova, and Fowler stand in silence.

BISHOP

What is the meaning of this? Some sort of a sick joke! Who are these people?

TERRY

Well it's not the "boy bishop" celebration.

GORDY

You must remember, Robert. It's in the gospels: "If a church member sins against you, first talk to the sinner privately. If the person doesn't listen to you, bring along two or three other members for a second conversation. If that doesn't work, the sinful member should be brought before the entire church." That's all we're doing.

DENIS FRANK

(Steps into the light and faces the bishop) You're full of surprises, Bishop Bergeron. You say you don't recognize these people? You should. They wrote to you, tried to talk to you, some pleaded with you and told you about their molesters and rapists.

You don't recognize these people? This is the mother of a boy named Kevin, who committed suicide because he couldn't deal with the shame of being raped by one of your priests. (Mrs. Lynch steps out of the shadows.)

And this is a woman who had to have an abortion after one of yours got her pregnant. (A woman steps into the light.) (Bergeron, is silent and stunned.)

(As Frank continues, one by one men and women step forward into a circle of light.) These are the people you allowed your priests to rape and sodomize.

These are the people you called liars and gagged to protect those priests.

These are the people whose innocence was taken away, who no one would believe. And when they came to you, you had your lawyers frighten and silence them with threats. These are the victims of your crimes Bishop Robert Bergeron. These are the people and children you sacrificed for the reputation of the Church and its clergy. The innocents you slaughtered!

You should remember me. Denis Frank. I wrote to you to tell you what Murtaugh had done to me. Your lawyers called me a drunk and said it was my word against a holy priest. These are the people who suffered in silence for years because they were afraid and ashamed. You called us dirty little liars who were ruining the name of the Church.

Now it's our turn to judge you. Now we want the voice that was silenced by the unspeakable acts of men of God who were supposed to protect our purity and innocence. (Lights fade on those who have come forward.)

I'll give you a shot at walking out of here, before we start videoing. But you must take a little quiz. Want to try that, your excellency? (Ties bishop's hands.)

BISHOP

Is this some sick stupid prank? If you think you can bully me or scare me, you're wrong. You do know that you will all be arrested for assault. If you thought our attorneys were scary before, you have no idea. I am a bishop of the Roman Catholic Church.

GORDY

Exactly. And we have something more in keeping with what might be called the "good ole days" of the Roman Catholic Church. All we're asking is that you take some responsibility; tell the truth, and it seems that the only way to do that is to tie you down – literally. Friendly persuasion, like the Inquisition you might say. And since we have some very learned classmates, we want to share this little session. You see, we heard some things about you and your priests that are shameful. And since this was the place where liars were sent, well, you know.

FRANCO

It's called the Rite of Degradation, used for errant clergy. And too bad stuff like this isn't used anymore. We've made some minor changes, like Latin to English, but it is right on! Remember the thing we did for the Boy Bishop? Well, that's how we start, all dressed up.

BISHOP

Franco, I'll have you fired from the college! And Wadhams I will make sure you land in jail! Fenton, I have lawyers. You're a judge, you know this can't be legal. Whatever you have in mind I demand you stop right now. You can't do this.

FENTON

I am a judge with some familiarity with Canon Law. Canon 1717 to be exact: Whenever the Ordinary, that's you, receives information, which has at least the semblance of truth, about an offense, he is to enquire carefully, either personally or through some suitable person, about the facts and circumstances, and about the imputability of the offense...

BISHOP

Fenton, I'm a bishop for God's sake!

GORDY

Let's leave God out of this for the time being, shall we?

117

BISHOP

I…. this is ridiculous!

GORDY

Do you know right from wrong?

(Silence)

BISHOP

Of course, I do!

GORDY

Then tell me what makes something wrong? Let me refresh your memory. There are some things so evil, that regardless of the intended consequences, are wrong. Then there are things, maybe like lying, or even killing, that can be right or wrong, depending on the situation or circumstance. Do you think the consequences of your lying matter?

BISHOP

This is absurd. What do you want from me? You can't do this to me.

DENIS FRANK

Yet, here we are. And we have judged that your actions were wrong and that you have protected evil men and perpetrated horrendous suffering. Your actions have sacrificed innocent children and their families. And to protect yourself and what you consider the best interest of your Church you lied to and slandered people who came to you for help.

BISHOP

I did what I thought was best. I have nothing to confess.

GORDY

We're not interested in "guilt" or some feeble attempt to apologize for years of hiding and protecting criminals, even excusing their behavior. Because the secret is, you were protecting yourselves and your great little "club."

BISHOP

And do you think you are going to accomplish anything by this fiasco?

DENIS FRANK

Personally, I'm interested in something called the "honest to God truth." And maybe all we really want is the satisfaction of dealing with you as a "whited sepulcher" who pretends he's not guilty for a whole lot of pain and suffering.

BISHOP

And dealing with me in this way exempts you from guilt? I have faithfully served the Church. That is my "greater good." I never did anything to these people.

GORDY

You always seem to have the right answers. No, you're right, you didn't do anything, but you **should have** when they asked for help, when they told you about Murtaugh and others like him.

BISHOP

I served my Church. I did what was best.

GORDY

On the contrary, I say, you served power and money, not Jesus and what he stands for. And we're not here to punish you, just to get at some truth. It's a judgment call. Some here might call you an "enabler." But the raw truth is that you are an "accomplice."

BISHOP

You're not God!

GORDY

Right there, Bobbo. I suspect he, or she, has a thing or two to say to you eventually. Didn't Jesus use some rough tactics to clean up the temple. You felt smug because you were morally justified to defend a Church you thought was being attacked. Lies cannot make us free. And your morality forgot the most important rule. Remember, about treating others.

TERRY

I wasn't present when Gordy called these guys. And I thought they were out of their freaking minds. But when we heard the stories some of these people had to tell, I knew someone had to do something. We knew the law wouldn't go after you. And we believed that the Church might conveniently "promote" you to some Vatican job, thus keeping you safely away from any prosecution. It was Terranova, Professor Marco, here who came up with this wonderful idea.

Real old Church. Right up your alley, a kind of exclusion and defrocking.

BISHOP

This is ridiculous. Let me out of here, now!

DENIS FRANK

All we want is an admission that you were complicit and allowed priests to violate the innocent and vulnerable.

BISHOP

I did what I thought was best. I had to protect the Church

DENIS FRANK

Just say 'through my fault, through my fault, through my most grievous fault.' Isn't that how it goes?

BISHOP

I have nothing to confess.

GORDY

Unfortunately, Robert Bergeron you have been found guilty on the testimony of these wounded witnesses. So now since you have professed to be such a faithful son of the Church, we only think it appropriate that we let her speak and deal with you.

BISHOP

You can't get away with this! I'll have you all arrested for kidnapping and assault! You've laid violent hands on God's anointed!

GORDY

Oh no. You came here of your own free will, to a class reunion. For drinking and fun. O'Malley can confirm that, you had an invitation! And, so far, **we** haven't even touched you. And you have chosen to ignore, silence or defame others here. As far as anybody knows you got drunk and had a bad dream.

(Fenton and the others move out of the light. Men and women emerge from the shadowed darkness of the crypt. Some carrying large lighted candles. They encircle Bergeron. They then move to form a semi-circle around him. This time he stands with a cope and miter on. The reunion group is now in shadows.)

BISHOP

(Shouting in panic) You can't do this. I AM the Church!

(Bergeron is gagged)

CHORUS OF VOICES

Robert Bergeron, led by the grossest of evil, you have ravaged the Church of God, stole its treasure for coercion and suppression of the truth and violently oppressed the poor of Christ especially the most innocent and vulnerable.

MALE

In our concern over this, we do not desire that you perish. For before the dread Judgment seat, we will all have to render an account to the Prince of Shepherds. But we admonish you, in accordance with the terrible warning of the words of Holy Scripture:

WOMAN

If thou dost not speak to warn and speak out to dissuade a wicked man from his wicked ways, I will hold you responsible... and we charge you with the words of Christ, himself: See that you do not despise one of these little ones, for their angels in heaven continually see the face of My Father.

CHORUS OF VOICES

Therefore, we have repeatedly called on you so that you might stop and prevent evil and pleaded that you speak out against evil men. But you, despising the salutary admonitions of the people of God, which you have offended, and led by the spirit of pride, have caused anguish, misery, enduring suffering and even death.

WOMAN

Therefore, let us take from the body of the Church this putrid and incurable member, so that the rest of the members of the body may not be poisoned by such a pestiferous disease and lying tongue.

MAN

He has despised our admonitions and our repeated exhortations; he would not amend himself and do penance; he has not reflected upon his guilt, nor has he confessed it; neither has he presented any excuse, nor did he ask for pardon.

CHORUS OF VOICES

But, with his heart hardened by power and pride, he continues to persevere in the same evil as before.

MRS. LYNCH

Wherefore by our judgment, we denounce Robert Bergeron, bishop, with all his accomplices and all his abettors and we see him separate him from the society of all Christians; and wish him excluded from the bosom of our Holy Mother the Church in Heaven and on earth; and we declare him - an abomination.

DENIS FRANK

By your false faithfulness to an institution you betrayed God's people whom you were ordained to serve and preserve in holiness.

MRS. LYNCH

By your imagined loyalty to the brotherhood of priests you corrupted the holiness of the Church and allowed sin to triumph. By your obsessive need to guard the Church from ignominious reproach you betrayed the truth of the Gospel you were to proclaim.

MEN'S VOICES

We judge you worthy of eternal fire with Satan and his angels and all the reprobates. So long as you will not amend yourself and do penance and make reparation to the Church which you have wounded and those who have suffered unspeakable ignominy because of you. We pray that your soul may be saved on the day of judgment.

ALL

So be it! Let it be so! This is our judgment! Amen! Amen!

(At this those carrying candles cast them to the floor. (Mrs. Lynch takes off gag from bishop) Then one by one men and women come forward to take episcopal regalia and then walk off stage.)

BISHOP

This is an outrage. A sacrilegious display of contempt for the Church!!!

MAN

(Takes off mitre and then walks off stage) We strip your head of this mitre, emblem of episcopal dignity, since you have befouled it by your misuse of authority!

(A large gospel book held by two women is slammed close in front of Bergeron.)

WOMEN

Give us back the Gospel. Since you have spurned its words and made yourself unworthy of moral teaching, we rightly deprive you of this office! (They carry to book off.)

MAN

(Grabs bishops hand and pulls off ring) We take away your ring, the sign of pure fidelity, because you have allowed the rape of God's own!

WOMAN

(With crosier (bishop's staff) in hand.) We take this shepherd's staff, because you have not exercised the office of correction and allowed devouring wolves to maim and kill those entrusted to you!

MAN

Once your hands and head were blessed by sacramental anointing for the good of God's holy people, we now mark you with dirt because you have fouled and mired that gift and your hands have become sullied with innocent blood. (Ashes are smeared across Bergeron's head and hands.)

WOMAN

(As the cope is removed and rips pectoral cross from around bishop's neck.) We leave you debased unclothed. Naked of all the things that gave you power.

(All leave the stage, except Denis Frank.)

DENIS FRANK

Power that you used to hide and protect predators, rapists, sick and hideous criminals who did unspeakable and repulsive things to children. And you were complicit in all the appalling and disgusting things they did. We wrote, we called, we begged you to do something! You said you were protecting the Church! (Bergeron remains silent. But faintly.)

BISHOP

Help me... please.

DENIS

Maybe now you know how it feels to be helpless, violated, dirty, powerless, naked and afraid. And no one will ever believe that this ever happened to you. You had too much to drink, fell asleep down here and had a nightmare. Who would believe that anyone had the colossal affrontery to treat you, a bishop, with anything but respect and fear? (Denis, releases Bergeron's hands.)

BISHOP

I'm a victim here. This is a serious abuse.

DENIS

We're all victims of something...or someone. Take your own advice, your excellency. Remember? "Nothing happened. Move on. The Church is counting on you. God's blessings." And by the way. None of this is on tape. There is no proof. And everybody, well...You remember so like you were fond of saying: "This **never** really happened. It couldn't have, I was in charge."

(Denis walks off into darkness and Bergeron is left standing alone on stage.)

(BLACKOUT)

(Spot on O'Malley dressed in civilian clothes.)

O'MALLEY

There really isn't an end to this story. As a trained therapist I am still seeing victims of clergy abuse. Some laws have changed but the Church seems incapable of dealing with the clergy perpetrators or hierarchy who protects them. Unhappily much of the same cover-up and deceit continues. You know, maybe the people of Ste. Pierre, in their own way, had a solution. Denis Frank told me about the incident at the seminary reunion. Bishop Bergeron kept silent about that evening and I saw that he got a promotion to one of the Vatican offices in Rome. I hope that he finds the kind of peace he once prayed for.

(BLACKOUT)

(CURTAIN)

CPSIA information can be obtained
at www.ICGtesting.com
Printed in the USA
LVHW081059211221
706793LV00005B/149